DINOBIBI

SPAIN

TRAVEL FOR KIDS

www.dinobibi.com

Author: Celia Jenkins
Editor: Kristy Elam
Illustrator: Jacqueline Cacho

CONTENTS

River Boy

Hola! Nice to meet you. My name is Rio, do you know what it means? In Spanish, the name Rio means 'river.' I've known this since I was a little boy, so I think my personality has grown to be like a river. Sometimes I can be calm and gentle. But usually, I'm fierce and wild! I like to run around and cause chaos, haha. Do you think names have meanings? I do. My madre's name is Alondra, which means lark. She can sing just like a bird!

An Extended Family

I've told you about my madre, but what about my padre? Well, what if I told you I have three fathers? You've be surprised, no? Well, it's a long story... Madre and Padre met when they were very young. They weren't married when I was born, and after a few years, they decided to split up. By the way, this isn't common for Spain! Most people get married before they have children and few people get divorced. But, like me, my parents like to be different!

4

My Family History

So, I was living with my madre and, eventually, she fell in love with and married another man. His name is Matias, and he's not like my father at all, but we get on well. So that's how I got my second padre! After many years of being a bachelor, my padre told us that he was gay. Madre says she wasn't surprised, only that it took him so long to figure it out! I love my padre whether he has a girlfriend or a boyfriend. At the moment his boyfriend is Natal, and so he's like my third padre. It seems very complicated, no? We're different than other families, but I love them all the same.

Oh, by the way, when Matias married my mother, I got a sister. Her name is Julina, and we don't talk very often. She's a few years older than me. I'm nearly twelve but she's seventeen, so she doesn't want to spent much time with me! Julina's mother died when she was little.

San Cayetano Chapel in Puebla de Sanabria, Spain.

Fun Fact
In Spain, about 67% of people are Catholic.

Changing Traditions in Spain

Another thing that makes my family different is that none of my family are religious. We don't go to church and don't believe in God. Actually, it's not so uncommon now. One in four people in Spain is non-religious. But in small villages like mine, there's often a higher population of religious people.

My step-father was born and raised in a small village called Puebla de Sanabria, where we live now. The village is in the province of Zamora, in the west of Spain. I spend most of my time here in Zamora, but I spend most of my holidays with my father in Toledo. Sometimes I visit Padre on the weekend, but it's a 3-hour drive to get to Toledo! I miss him so much. But he's busy with his work, so I know it's not possible to see him often.

Aerial View of Puebla de Sanabria.

Small Town Boy

Matias and Padre are different in so many ways! Matias is one of the only doctors in Puebla de Sanabria. Being a doctor is one of the most respected jobs in Spain, and the pay is very good. When people see me, they say "That's Rio, the doctor's son," since my town in so small. People know him and me! As such, Madre doesn't need to work. She's enjoying her life as a homemaker now!

By comparison, Padre has one of the least respected jobs in Spain! He's a journalist for one of the popular newspapers in Toledo. People don't respect journalists these days, so he doesn't make a lot of money. But Padre has an entrepreneurial spirit. He makes money by writing a blog on his website. It's all about LGBTQ rights in Spain, and how people's attitudes are changing towards gay people. I'm proud of my padre and the work he does.

Before we continue our trip, I would like to know more about you. Can you please complete this little questionnaire for me?

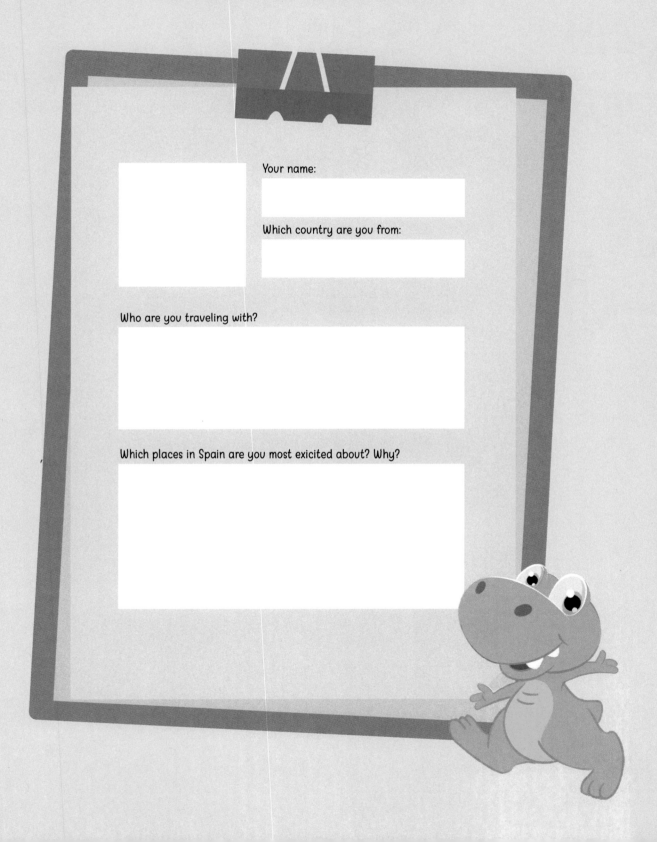

Your name:

Which country are you from:

Who are you traveling with?

Which places in Spain are you most exicited about? Why?

France

Portugal

How do You Spend Your Pocket Money?

Madre just gave me my pocket money for the week. Do you get pocket money? Even though my step-father has a good job, I don't get nearly as much pocket money as my friends do! Some of my friends receive €5 or €10 every week. They're so lucky! Matias earns a lot of money, but he's strict when he comes to sharing it. Each week, I get what he calls a base rate of €2. If I want more than that, I need to earn it. Madre gives me an extra €1 each time I do a chore around the house. For example, if I do something like sweeping all the floors, doing the laundry, washing the dishes, or cleaning the toilet, I get an extra €1. This week I did three chores so I've got €5 in total. As you can probably guess, €5 doesn't buy very much!

Whenever I get my pocket money, I divide it in half. I put half into my piggy bank and half I can spend on something sweet. I've got a sweet tooth and Madre doesn't usually buy sweets to have at home. This week I only have €2.5 to spend. But it's enough to get a little something. If it's a hot day and I want an ice cream, gelato, or ice lolly, those cost around €2 to €4. I also use my pocket money to buy candy or chocolate. There isn't such a big variety here as in other places. Padre once took me for a holiday to the UK. I was amazed how many types of chocolate bars they had there! In Spain, people don't eat so much chocolate, so we don't have a variety of bars to choose from.

Fun Fact
Children in Spain get between €5 and €10 of pocket money per week.

Stone houses of Puebla de Sanabria.

Village Views

I always go to the same shop to buy my weekend treats. Puebla de Sanabria is a small town and I can walk to the shop in under ten minutes. It's a very traditional village with stone walls and cobbled streets. One of our neighbours, Mr. Sanchez, has the flag of Spain in his garden. Would you recognise our flag? It has two red stripes and a yellow stripe in the middle. There's also a coat of arms on the big yellow stripe, but sometimes you see the flag without it.

The village is built on a hillside, and there are amazing views as I walk to the shop. I like to look down at the town and see the river below and the blue sky above. Because my name is Rio, I have a special interest in rivers! In Puebla de Sanabria, two rivers meet — Rio Castra and Rio Tera. The Tera River is a tributary of the River Esla, and it's been a designated Special Area of Conservation since 2015 because it's the home of 24 species of the European Union Nature Directives, so it's ecologically important.

Rivers of Spain

Spain has around 1,800 rivers, did you know that? Sí, it's true. I know all about rivers so you can trust me on this point! What I find most interesting is that out of the five main rivers in Spain, four of them flow southwards and west-wards. If you look at a map of the big rivers in Spain, those four rivers look like stripes across our country. The longest is the River Tajo which is 1,007 km (625 miles) long. I know this one well because the river passes by Toledo, where my padre lives.

Summer Camp

I've been more interested in Spanish geography since I went to summer camp last year. It was a mountain camp where I spent two weeks learning about nature and doing things like swimming in the lake, building camp fires, and climbing trees.

I made friends with boys and girls from all over Spain. I met a boy called Diego who comes from Madrid — that's the biggest metropolitan area of Spain. A lot of the other campers were from Madrid! There was a girl called Sierra who was from Seville, which is the largest city in Andalusia, in the south. I also met a boy called Manuel who was from Andalusia, but he was from Marbella. There were many campers from Barcelona, too. Of course, I was the only camper from Puebla de Sanabria!

Well, I'm almost at the shops now, so I just need to decide what to spend my pocket money on. Hmm, it's a warm day... so perhaps I'll choose an ice cream!

WEATHER IN SPAIN

Rain in Gijon, in the Atlantic coast of Spain.

The Land of Winter Sun

Buenos días, good morning! Wow, it's hot today. I could do with an ice cream. How about you? What do you like in the hot, sunny weather? I like to go swimming whenever I can. Or perhaps spend time by the river, my name sake. I remember spending time with Madre by the river, and sometimes I'd hide from her. She'd call out, "Where's Rio?" and then I'd jump out, point at the river and say, "There it is!" Haha, ok, I'm not much of a comedian, I know!

I bet you think that it's always hot and sunny in Spain, right? I bet you think we eat ice cream every day and spend all our free time at the beach. Actually, we get cold weather in Spain, too. And remember Spain is a big country. It's not the same weather across all of Spain. Some places in Spain are warm even in winter. That's why tourists from countries in northern Europe, like the UK, come to Spain at Christmas for some 'winter sun'.

Fun Fact
Spain is the most climatically diverse country in Europe and is within the 10 most climatically diverse countries in the world.

The port city of Santander in the North coast of Spain.

The North of Spain

In the north of Spain, the weather is temperate, and we get a lot of rainfall. The south is temperate too, but it's hot and dry. Mainly, Spain has a Mediterranean climate. In the northeast, where Spain shares a border with France, we have highs of 20°C (68 °F) in the summer, and lows of 6°C (43 °F) in the winter. The northwest is a little warmer, with temperatures averaging 21°C (69 °F) in the summer. The south, of course, is the warmest. In the summer, average temperatures reach 25°C (77 °F.) The center of Spain can be colder in the winter.

We can also have very cold weather in Spain. It's easy to understand when you remember that we have mountains. It can get very cold at the top of a mountain! The coldest temperature recorded in Spain was –32 °C (–26 °F) at Lake Estangento, Lleida, in the west of Catalonia in 1956. Many of the coldest temperatures happened in the 1940's – 1970's. In recent years, it's been rare to have extremely cold temperature. On Christmas Eve in 2001, the temperature in Torremocha de Jiloca dropped to −25.2 °C (−13.4 °F.) Brrr!

Aigüestortes i Estany de Sant Maurici National Park.

Best Time of Year

In Spain, there are two months that I call the 'golden months.' These are the times when the weather is warm but not too hot. Also, it's dry and doesn't rain very much. The first one is May, and the second one is October. My birthday is in May, and it's a great time for a celebration after the cold winter and spring. May is when it starts to feel like summer, but it's not super-hot yet. By the end of August, I get tired of the sun and the heat! So, if you're wondering when is the best time to visit Spain, I recommend coming in May!

Girona Flower Festival held in the month of May.

Feeling Hot, Hot, Hot

Everyone thinks that coming to the south of Spain will be an amazing, tropical holiday. But it isn't for everyone. If you haven't been to a warm place before, you should think carefully about coming to a hot country in the summertime. I have a distant cousin who lives in Sweden, which is a cold country! She really wanted to experience a warmer climate so she visited Spain in August. She found it very hard to have an active, enjoyable time. Every day she got too tired to visit places and just wanted to lie around all day. I don't think it was a good choice for her to come in the middle of summer!

It's nice to be somewhere sunny, though. My cousin told me that, in Sweden, they don't see the sunshine very often in the winter. I'd find that so depressing. In Spain, we have around 350 hours of sunshine in the month of July. Even in the winter, in December or January, we have about 120 or 130 hours of sunshine per month. It rains the least in July and August, too. The rainiest months are November, December, and April. But even then, it doesn't rain so much. Even in the rainiest times, we have just one week of rainy days in the whole month. So, it's not that bad!

HISTORY OF SPAIN

Ruins of a Roman amphitheater in Cartagena, Spain.

Spanish History Week

Hola! How are you today? I just got back from school, and I feel frazzled! We have a special event at school this month. Each week we focus on a different theme and do special lessons on that topic. This week it's Spanish History Week. Every day we've been learning about different periods of Spanish history. I like history but it's tiring to study it every day! There are so many details about different eras. Anyway, I thought you might like to hear about some of things I've learned.

A long time ago, before the Romans came, Spain was called Hispania. The two main tribes in Hispania were the Celts and the Iberians. Later, the Greeks and the Phoenicians came to Hispania. The Phoenicians were a Mediterranean civilization that mostly came from Lebanon. The Basques were a people living in the Pyrenees mountain area. I think things were quite peaceful between tribes at that time. But then the Romans came!

Fun Fact
The Romans invaded Spain during the Second Punic War, roughly 210-205 BC.

15

General Hamilcar Barca established Carthaginian authority in Iberia, Southwestern Spain. Some sources believe that the city of Barcelona got its old name "Barcino" from the Barcid family of Hamilcar.

Punic War

It took about 200 years for the Romans to take over the whole of Hispania, but once they had control, they reigned for six centuries! The cultures of the Celts and Iberians slowly disappeared as people became more Romanised. Across Hispania, people started to speak the same language and Christianity was introduced in the 1st century. But the rule of the Romans wasn't to last. The Roman Empire started to weaken, and other civilizations invaded Spain.

Fun Fact

After losing in the first Punic War, General Hamilcar Barca, re-established Cathaginian authority in Iberia, leading to the Roman invasion of Spain in the Second Punic War.

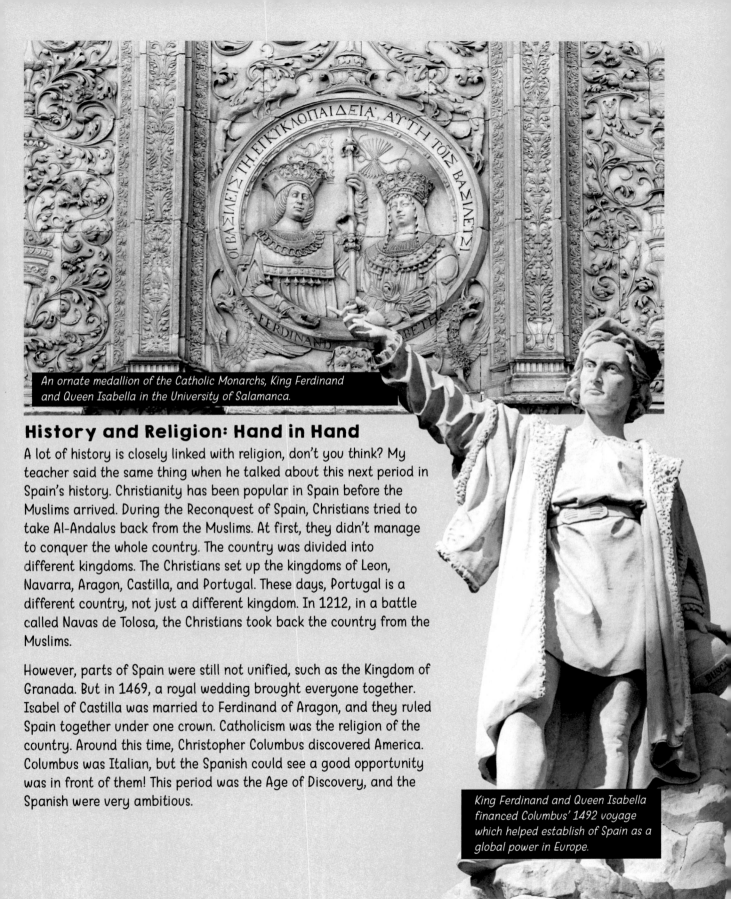

An ornate medallion of the Catholic Monarchs, King Ferdinand and Queen Isabella in the University of Salamanca.

History and Religion: Hand in Hand

A lot of history is closely linked with religion, don't you think? My teacher said the same thing when he talked about this next period in Spain's history. Christianity has been popular in Spain before the Muslims arrived. During the Reconquest of Spain, Christians tried to take Al-Andalus back from the Muslims. At first, they didn't manage to conquer the whole country. The country was divided into different kingdoms. The Christians set up the kingdoms of Leon, Navarra, Aragon, Castilla, and Portugal. These days, Portugal is a different country, not just a different kingdom. In 1212, in a battle called Navas de Tolosa, the Christians took back the country from the Muslims.

However, parts of Spain were still not unified, such as the Kingdom of Granada. But in 1469, a royal wedding brought everyone together. Isabel of Castilla was married to Ferdinand of Aragon, and they ruled Spain together under one crown. Catholicism was the religion of the country. Around this time, Christopher Columbus discovered America. Columbus was Italian, but the Spanish could see a good opportunity was in front of them! This period was the Age of Discovery, and the Spanish were very ambitious.

King Ferdinand and Queen Isabella financed Columbus' 1492 voyage which helped establish of Spain as a global power in Europe.

Spanish Conquistador Hernán Cortés .

Spaniards Abroad

Have you heard of the Conquistadors? The name comes from the word 'to conquer' and describes a group of people who wanted to be masters of the world. They sailed to different places, far beyond the reaches of Europe. The Conquistadors claimed many places for Spain in the 16th – 18th centuries. One famous Conquistador was Hernán Cortés. He waged a war against the Aztec Empire. Another famous empire that fell to the Conquistadors was the Inca Empire. The armies of Spain had armour and weapons that made them unbeatable to the native tribes they were attacking. The treasures they found were incredible, and they wanted it all for themselves.

The Aztec and Inca Empires had hordes of gold and silver which the Spanish stole.

The Spanish Conquistadors were greedy, ruthless, and cruel. They killed thousands of men, women, and children to take their gold and steal their land. Sometimes they asked for ransoms of gold to let the natives live but then killed the natives anyway. It's a dark period of Spain's history. The Cholula Massacre and the Temple Massacre at the Festival of Toxcatl were two of the worst atrocities. The Conquistadors often fought each other, too. While the leaders took home a lot of gold, the average soldiers didn't get much.

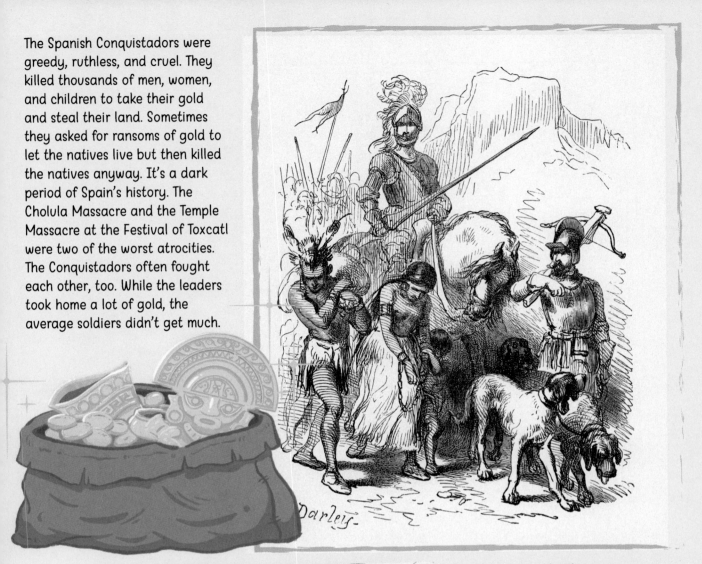

It seems to me like these guys were really dumb! They were so hungry for gold that believed fantasy stories to make them wealthy. Many Conquistadors genuinely searched for the fountain of youth, as well as the city of El Dorado, but of course they never found either of them! The most tragic thing is that it was all for nothing. The Conquistadors wanted to control areas all over the world, but after they'd killed the native tribes and stolen their goods, they couldn't even keep leadership of those places! In 1898, Spain lost the last of its colonies.

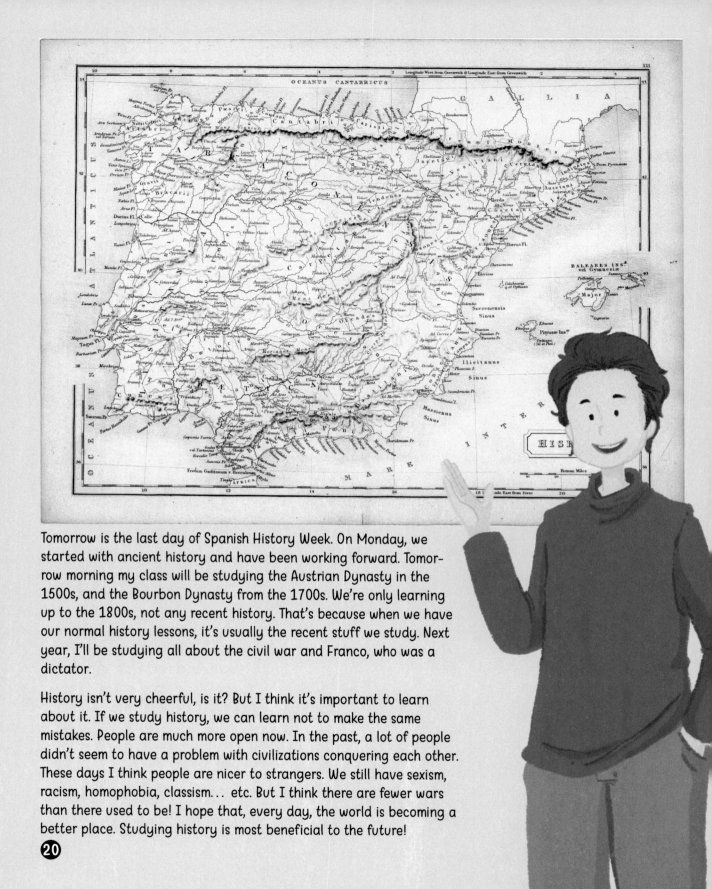

Tomorrow is the last day of Spanish History Week. On Monday, we started with ancient history and have been working forward. Tomorrow morning my class will be studying the Austrian Dynasty in the 1500s, and the Bourbon Dynasty from the 1700s. We're only learning up to the 1800s, not any recent history. That's because when we have our normal history lessons, it's usually the recent stuff we study. Next year, I'll be studying all about the civil war and Franco, who was a dictator.

History isn't very cheerful, is it? But I think it's important to learn about it. If we study history, we can learn not to make the same mistakes. People are much more open now. In the past, a lot of people didn't seem to have a problem with civilizations conquering each other. These days I think people are nicer to strangers. We still have sexism, racism, homophobia, classism... etc. But I think there are fewer wars than there used to be! I hope that, every day, the world is becoming a better place. Studying history is most beneficial to the future!

Park Güell, Carmel Hill, Barcelona.

A Garden of Local Wonders

Hola! How are you today? I'm taking a rest because I've had a busy morning. I've been helping my neighbour, Mr. Sanchez, in his garden. Mr. Sanchez is in his eighties but he loves to do gardening every day. We only have a small garden, but Mr. Sanchez has a massive one. If I have time on the week-ends, I like to work in his garden. It helps me to earn a bit more pocket money. Not only that, but Mr. Sanchez is very knowledgeable. He has been teaching me more about the natural world. I think Mr. Sanchez would like me to be a gardener in the future! He says I'm a natural. But I'm too young to think about that! I just like to be outside and doing something useful.

21

Lovely Local Plants

Mr. Sanchez says we are lucky to live in Spain. Our country has more different types of vascular plants than any other country in Europe. I'm not really sure what a vascular plant is. Mr. Sanchez uses a lot of special garden words that I don't understand! But I think it's something to do with how the plant spreads water and minerals around the plant. Anyway, Spain has eight or nine thousand different species of vascular plants. Isn't that incredible? I wonder how many of those Mr. Sanchez can name!

Fun Fact

Between 20 and 25% of Spain's vascular plants are endemic to the country. That means that they're indigenous to Spain — they come from Spain.

The Alhambra is a fortress complex in Granada, Andalucia, Sain. The place hold several garden attractions like the Jardín de la Sultana and Patio de la Acequia.

Mr. Sanchez isn't just interested in practical gardening. I think, when he was younger, his job was to research the history of Spain's natural environment. He said Spain used to have a lot of forests but now there aren't so many. A lot of Spain is covered in maquis. That's the name for dense shrubland that has a lot of evergreen shrubs, herbaceous plants, and scatterings of trees. The types of tree you see depend on the soil. In sandy soil, you can see types of pine tree, whereas in areas with more limestone you can see juniper, oak and Aleppo pine. The north-western coast, near where I live, has forests of trees such as ash, maple, lime, common oak, chestnut, elm, and hazel.

Flowers and Vegetables

Mr. Sanchez grows a few vegetables in his garden. He lives alone so he doesn't need to grow much food. He likes to grow different types of flowers. He said his garden is truly Spanish, because he prefers to grow Spanish flowers rather than imported ones. He said "Why would I grow flowers from other countries? I live in Spain, so the best flowers to grow here are Spanish ones!" Oh, he makes me laugh. Mr. Sanchez is quite old fashioned. But he does have a very lovely garden.

Fun Fact

Traditional Spanish gardens are based on Persian gardens and Islamic gardens. These are often symmetrical with a pond or fountain in the middle. Water and stonework are very important, with flora adding color around the edges.

Beautiful Blooms

The official flower of Spain is the pomegranate flower. The color is very rich, like a blood orange. Pomegranate flowers have so many petals. They look like the ruffles on a flamenco dancer's skirt. A similar flower is the red carnation, which is smaller but has similar petals. Carnations come in different colors, but Mr. Sanchez likes the red flowers best. He says they have different meanings. Red ones mean love and passion, white ones are for purity and good luck, and the pink carnations mean gratitude and are good presents for mothers.

I like his lantana flowers which are by the patio. Lantana love the sunshine, so it's a good idea to put them somewhere warm. Mr. Sanchez grows lantana in many different colors; lilac, yellow, orange, and red. At the end of the garden is a wall of color from the bougainvillea. The bush is thick with flowers and needs to be pruned often. Madre loves these flowers too, but our garden isn't big enough for them — they'd swamp it! Our garden doesn't have a pond like our neighbours do. Mr. Sanchez doesn't keep fish in his pond, just water lilies. They're pretty but they don't last very long. But when one water lily dies, there's often another one to take its place.

Small Spanish Creatures

Sometimes Mr. Sanchez tells me about animals, too. But he doesn't like animals! Sometimes little pests come into his garden and eat the plants. Mr. Sanchez does his best to keep the wild animals out of his garden, but he doesn't mind the birds. At the end of the garden, by the bougainvillea, is a small bird table where he puts out bird seed.

An animal I've never seen before is the Pyrenean desman. They're semiaquatic, which means they spend some of their time living in water and some of it on land. A desman is like a shrew or a mole. Their size is about 11 – 14 cm long (4.3 to 5.5 inches.) They look so funny! They have long noses and webbed feet, so they look a bit like a cross between a mouse and a duck! Where I live, in the north-western side of Spain, is great place to spot a desman, but I never have.

Fun Fact

The Pyrenean desman is good at swimming and climbing. It uses its long, sensitive nose to detect its prey under mud. It can even close off its nostrils to prevent water and mud from getting in!

Something I see a lot of are rabbits and hares. These are particularly disliked by Mr. Sanchez! One year, a rabbit came into his garden and ate all his carrots! I don't think he grows carrots any more. Sometimes I see squirrels, rats, and moles if I go into the countryside. By the river I can often see otters, too. But these are all small animals. In Spain, we have bigger carnivores, but they don't usually come near where humans live. One day I'd love to see a lynx. The Eurasian lynx can be found all over Europe. The lynx is a solitary animal, so you're unlikely to see two together, unless it's the mating season. They have short tails and beautiful coats covered in black spots. I particularly like their ears which have long hairs on the tips.

I'm interested in animals, but I don't think I want a pet. It's too much work! Also, because I go to visit my padre quite often, it would be difficult to travel with a pet. Perhaps when I'm older I'll consider having a pet, but I don't want anything boring like a cat or dog. I think I'd prefer to have an exotic bird or maybe a reptile. That would be far more interesting to me!

Your Birthday - The Day it's Okay to Hit

Hey there! How are you? As for me, I'm not looking forward to today. Do you remember I said that I had a big sister? Well, today is Juliana's birthday. My step-sister will be eighteen years old and is having a party at our house. She's turning eighteen which means she'll be an adult, but she doesn't act like one! Juliana and all her friends seem to like things that little children like! Like most of Europe, in Spain you're allowed to purchase alcohol once you're eighteen. So, I thought Juliana and her friends would want to go to a bar. But they don't want to do that. She wants to have a birthday party at our house and play party games. Actually, you're allowed to drink alcohol at any age in Spain — the law is only about buying alcohol. On special occasions, Madre lets me have a little wine at dinner time, but I don't like it very much.

26

So yes, all of Juliana's friends will be coming to our house. Do you know what a piñata is? A piñata is a popular toy to have at children's birthday parties. It's made from cardboard and covered in brightly colored paper. You hang the piñata in a tree or somewhere high, and then you have to hit it with a stick. The idea is to make it break open and all the sweets inside will fall out. Oh, and you have to be blindfolded which makes it more difficult. Anyway, Juliana is having a piñata shaped like a unicorn. Isn't that silly? I think unicorns are for little children, not eighteen-year olds! But Juliana really loves unicorns. She's having a unicorn shaped birthday cake, too.

Fun Fact

The piñata is popular in Spain, but it's believed to have originated in either China or Mexico. People these days have piñatas at birthday parties all over the world.

Quinceañera

Everyone is making out like this is a really special birthday for her. But Juliana already had a special birthday party. In Spain, when girls turn fifteen years old they have a special party called Quinceañera. This event symbolizes the coming of age when a girl becomes a woman. At the party, the birthday girl can wear a formal dress that's usually very expensive and her presents are often expensive jewelry.

Spanish Customs

A lot of our customs and traditions in Spain have links with religion. Spain used to be a very religious country, and Christianity is to thank for many of our customs. One of our biggest festivals is Semana Santa. It means Holy Week and the festival happens in the week before Easter. Across the country there are parades and parties, and different regions of Spain will dedicate the celebrations to different saints. But some of the festivities don't have much to do with saints! There's always a big bonfire we go to and a firework display. In some of the bigger towns they have beauty contests during Semana Santa, which doesn't have anything to do with religion at all!

Semana Santa procession in Magala, Spain.

Running of the Bulls

Do you know much about this bull sport in Spain? It's a bit of a hot topic because many people protest against it. They say its unkind and cruel to the animals. San Fermín is the name of a week-long festival we have in Spain. In English, it's called the Running of the Bulls. People know a lot about bull fighting, but this isn't a fight, although it sometimes takes place after there has been bullfighting. At the Running of the Bulls, people run through the narrow streets in front of the bulls. There are usually between six and ten bulls, but maybe more. Of course, the bulls can run much faster than humans can! The bulls try to overtake the humans which can cause accidents.

The festival originates from when the cattle would be transported from the fields (where they bred and raised) to the bullring (where they will be killed). It started because some of the young cattle men decided to run alongside the bulls to show how brave they were. Now it's a major event and, though it's mostly popular with Spanish people, others come from all over the world to watch or join in. The bull running in Pamplona is the most popular event in Spain. The San Fermín festival is held in early July. Every day of the festival there is bull running at 8am in the morning. You have to be eighteen years old to take part and can't have drunk any alcohol. Hey, maybe now that Juliana is eighteen, I should recommend she take part! Haha! No, she'd hate that. But she could take part if she wanted. 1974 was the first time that women were permitted to run in the event. But it's mostly men that take part.

The festival originates from when the cattle would be transported from the fields (where they bred and raised) to the bullring (where they will be killed). It started because some of the young cattle men decided to run alongside the bulls to show how brave they were. Now it's a major event and, though it's mostly popular with Spanish people, others come from all over the world to watch or join in. The bull running in Pamplona is the most popular event in Spain.

The San Fermín festival is held in early July. Every day of the festival there is bull running at 8am in the morning. You have to be eighteen years old to take part and can't have drunk any alcohol. Hey, maybe now that Juliana is eighteen, I should recommend she take part! Haha! No, she'd hate that. But she could take part if she wanted. 1974 was the first time that women were permitted to run in the event. But it's mostly men that take part.

I think the festival is strange, but I don't see why there's so much opposition. People say that the bulls get stressed out and could even die from the trauma of the event. But if you look at the statistics, there have been far more humans that have been killed in the event! I sometimes watch it on television and, despite the danger, people seem to love it. Those who run in the race say they feel like heroes and it's one of the best experiences of their lives. I don't think I'd ever want to take part, but perhaps I'll go to Pamplona one day to watch it.

Christmas decorations in Madrid, Spain.

Have You Put Out Your Shoes?

What's your favorite national holiday? Mine is definitely Christmas. The thing I like about Christmas is that everybody is celebrating. Birthdays are just for one person but at Christmas we can all have fun. Perhaps you think that Christmas is the same all over the world? I don't think so. Let me tell you about Spanish Christmas traditions, and you can compare it to your own Christmas celebrations.

One of the most famous things to do with Christmas is Santa Claus, right? In Spain, we have something different. Of course, these days we usually celebrate with Father Christmas instead, but traditionally, Spanish people would be more interested in Olentzero, which is actually a Basque tradition. Remember that Basque country is an area that's both in France and Spain, so the Basque people are a bit different. Anyway, Olentzero is very similar to Santa Claus. He comes to visit on December 24th and brings presents for good children. Olentzero doesn't wear a special suit — he is usually wearing peasants' rags and smoking a pipe. His name means something like 'the time of the good ones' which is about bringing presents to good children.

The Magi

Someone else who brings presents to children at Christmas time are the three kings. In the nativity story, there are three kings who bring gifts to the baby Jesus. Do you know the names of the kings? Their names were Melchior, Gaspar, and Baltazar. They say that each of the Magi (that's another word for Three Kings) are representing different continents: Melchior represents Europe, Gaspar represents Asia, and Africa is represented by Balthasar. We call the three kings Reyes Magos. But they don't bring their gifts on Christmas Day; they bring them on the 5th of January. Traditionally, it's not a Christmas stocking we leave for them to put presents in, but a pair of shoes!

Spaniards always look forward to beléns at Christmas time. Do you have a nativity scene in your house or school? Beléns comes from the word Bethlehem, and it means a nativity, but it's no ordinary nativity. A beléns is often very elaborate — not just the holy family, the kings, and the shepherds, but sometimes the scene includes a whole town with different figures. You can see big nativities in shop windows where the figures are life-sized. There's always a big one in the town square people enjoy looking at. Because we live in a small, traditional house we don't have room for a large beléns. However, I always help Mr. Sanchez to arrange his nativity in the front garden of his house.

If you're a Christian, perhaps you go to Midnight Mass on Christmas Eve? In Spain we call Midnight Mass the La Misa Del Gallo, which means the Mass of the Rooster. But as I told you, my family isn't religious so we don't go to La Misa Del Gallo. One Christmas tradition we do take part in is El Gordo. It means 'fat one.' Can you guess what it is? It's quite a funny name for a Christmas tradition, no? It's to do with the lottery. Every year since 1812, there has been a huge lottery jackpot at Christmas time in Spain. The Spanish Christmas lottery, which we call Sorteo Extraordinario de Navidad, is the biggest lottery draw in the world. It's true! Almost everyone in the country plays it!

Does your country have any funny Christmas traditions? Spain has some that I think are pretty weird! The first one is the tradition of fire jumping. It's an old tradition where people jump over a burning fire as it's supposed to bring them good luck. I don't think it would be very lucky if they landed on the fire! What with the tradition of running with the bulls and jumping over fires, you probably think the Spanish love doing dangerous things! In Galicia, a region of northwest Spain, not far from the province of Zamora where I live, they have a special Christmas tradition. It's a bit strange, though! It's about a coal miner named El Apalpador. He goes around feeling the tummies of children to check if they've been eating properly. If the children haven't been eating well, he will give them a sweet treat, like some chestnuts. I don't think I'd want a strange man to feel my tummy, even if I do get a chestnut in return!

Christmas Food

Do you want to know what we eat at Christmas? We don't have Christmas cake or Christmas pudding, but we have something similar. It's called Roscón de Reyes which means the ring of the kings. We eat it at Epiphany, the same time that the three kings bring us presents. The ring is a sweet bread in a ring shape. I'm sure you guessed that! The top is decorated with cherries, almonds, candied fruits, figs, and sometimes some icing sugar or whipped cream. It's traditional to bake the bread with a small figurine of the baby Jesus inside. Whoever finds the baby Jesus is blessed, but not if they take a bite from it! Haha.

Do you eat turkey on Christmas day? We don't, but we do have a special meal. There isn't a typical Christmas dish my family chooses — at Christmas, we always do something different. A popular choice at Christmas in Spain is seafood. A lobster or prawn platter might be the central part of a Christmas meal, or we might have seafood in a soup or stew. Another good choice is lamb or roast suckling pig. Mmm, my mouth is watering just thinking about all this delicious food!

Seafood Paella

Spanish Cuisine

One of the best things about having a stay-at-home mum is that we have such delicious food for dinner! Before Madre met my step-father, we didn't eat such interesting food. Madre had to work long hours after she split up with Padre, but now she has a wealthy husband, Madre can take it easy. Madre and Matias have a traditional relationship. He goes to work and earns the money. She stays at home and cooks and cleans the house. Matias says he isn't a good cook, but he's a fussy eater. He doesn't like foreign food and wants my mother to make him traditional Spanish dishes. Juliana prefers Spanish dishes too, so my mother spends a lot of time in the kitchen making delicious food.

Some Spanish dishes are famous, but there are others that I'm sure you haven't heard of. Most people are familiar with paella. Can you pronounce it? Some people say pay-la which is wrong! To pronounce it properly, you should say pie-ay-yah. The 'L' sound is different to what you imagine, no? Anyway, I'm sure you've heard of paella. It's a rice dish that comes from Valencia. You use short grain rice and serve the dish hot. We cook the dish in a special dish, and traditionally you would put this big pot on the table and everyone would eat out of it. Paella is a good dish for sharing as you can make a big quantity all at once. Seafood paella (with prawns, clams, lobster, and cuttlefish) is my favorite and the one my mother usually makes.

Fun Fact
The biggest paella ever cooked was made by a Valencian restaurateur called Juan Galbis. The dish fed over 100,000 people.

Sweets for Breakfast

Something else I guess you've heard of is churros. A churro is a noodle of choux pastry which is deep fried and then dipped either in chocolate or sugar with cinnamon. They're a popular snack to have with coffee around the world, but in Spain we usually have them for breakfast. If you have them for breakfast, churros are served with café con leche, which means coffee with milk. You dip the churro into the hot coffee, and it soaks up the delicious flavours of the drink. But as you can guess, this breakfast is quite unhealthy, so we only have it a few times a year for a special treat.

Churros

Patatas Brava

Calamares

Tiny Tapas Temptations

Potato is a popular staple in Spanish food. If you've ever been for tapas (which, by the way, means a small snack-sized plate of food, and you can order many tapas dishes to make a whole mean) then you've probably heard of patatas bravas. This dish consists of potato cubes cooked in oil so they're soft on the inside and crunchy on the outside. Patatas bravas is served with a tomato sauce drizzled over the top, and sometimes it's spicy. Croquetas is another popular potato tapas dish. The potato is mixed with another ingredient like fish, meat or cheese, and deep fried in breadcrumbs.

If you get tapas, you should get a mix of different dishes, not just potato cooked in different ways! I like calamares — these are deep fried rings of squid. When cooked right, the squid will be soft and just a little bit chewy. If it's cooked badly, the squid will be like rubber. A bowl of cold olives is a must for tapas, too. Empanadillas are little pastries filled with meat or vegetables. Queso con anchoas is a dish of cheese and anchovies. Albondigas are delicious meatballs. Mmm, I'm getting hungry thinking about all the mouth-watering tapas dishes in Spain! The nice thing about tapas is that you can try several different things. It's a good idea to get at least three tapas plates per person. So, if you're a family of four, you can order twelve different things! Tapas is a popular bar snack for people to nibble while they have a drink in a bar.

Matias's favorite dish is fabada asturiana. This popular food is a bean stew which you can buy it ready in a can, but Madre always makes it fresh for us. In the winter, we eat this dish at least once a week. In Spain, you eat your main meal at lunchtime, not at dinner time. It's so nice to have a hearty, warming dish like fabada asturiana in the middle of a cold day. It's a meaty stew made with bacon or pork shoulder.

Fabada Asturiana

Gazpacho

My step-sister Juliana doesn't do much cooking but she often makes gazpacho. It's a Spanish soup made mainly from tomatoes. In the summer people eat gazpacho every week, sometimes every day, because the soup is best served cold and is refreshing when the weather is warm. Juliana also makes Tortilla Española which means 'Spanish omelette.' It's quite simple, so even I can make it! Eggs, potato, onions... that's it. Of course, you don't have to make a basic omelette. I like to experiment and put other ingredients into it, such as chorizo, mushroom, ham, and peppers. But you have to be careful because if you add too many things, the omelette won't hold together. These aren't like English omelettes that look soggy and lumpy. A Spanish omelette is more like a cake. It's thick and has a smooth round shape from the frying pan.

My favourite dish that Madre makes is pollo al ajillo. It means chicken and garlic, and it's absolutely delicious. You fry big pieces of garlic in oil, then take out the garlic and add the chicken. Then when the chicken is cooked you put the garlic back in with some rosemary and white wine and thyme... it's a great dish for a special occasion. Everyone thinks their mother or grandmother makes the best pollo al ajillo, but they're wrong — my mother makes the best one!

Pollo al Ajillo

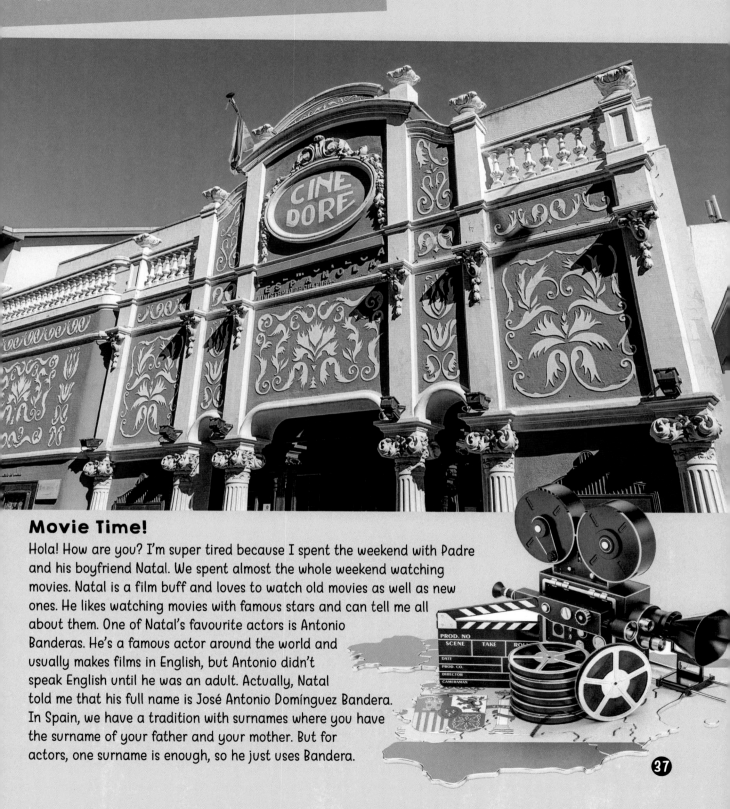

Movie Time!

Hola! How are you? I'm super tired because I spent the weekend with Padre and his boyfriend Natal. We spent almost the whole weekend watching movies. Natal is a film buff and loves to watch old movies as well as new ones. He likes watching movies with famous stars and can tell me all about them. One of Natal's favourite actors is Antonio Banderas. He's a famous actor around the world and usually makes films in English, but Antonio didn't speak English until he was an adult. Actually, Natal told me that his full name is José Antonio Domínguez Bandera. In Spain, we have a tradition with surnames where you have the surname of your father and your mother. But for actors, one surname is enough, so he just uses Bandera.

37

Antonio Banderas started acting in the early 1980s. He didn't make films in English until the 90s. This weekend I watched one of his early English films called *"The Mask of Zorro"*, made in 1998. The character played by Banderas is from Spanish California, so it is fitting that he has a Spanish accent! I'd seen him in other movies before, but those movies are for kids. They're called the *"Spy Kids"* movies, and they're older than me but I still like watching them, even if the special effects don't look good now. Oh, and have you seen the movie *"Shrek"*? Antonio Banderas does the voice of *"Puss in Boots"*!

Another Spanish actor, or should I say actress, is Penélope Cruz. Just like Antonio Banderas, she doesn't use both her surnames for her work, because her full name is Penélope Cruz Sánchez. She started working as a model when she was a teenager and became an actress just one year later. Actually, she also spent time trying to be a dancer but ended up as an actress. Just like Banderas, she made Spanish movies first but then changed to making more films in English.

In 2001, Penélope Cruz was twice nominated for the Golden Raspberry Award for Worst Actress, which isn't something an actress would like to win!

Wax figure of Penelope Cruz in GrAvin MontrAal, at the Montreal Eaton Centre in Montreal, Canada.

Natal isn't just interested in actors. He also knows about film directors. Natal's favourite Spanish director is Alejandro Amenábar. I don't know why because this guy hasn't made that many films. I think he's only made five or six proper films. His most famous film is probably The Others, which he made in 2001. It's a horror movie so Padre won't let me watch it. Natal says that Padre is being too strict, but I don't mind too much because I don't think I'd like a scary movie. Another film in English made by Alejandro Amenábar is called Regression.

The "Nobility of Time" sculpture by Salvador Dali.

Artistic Interests

I like watching films with my dad but I'm not a total movie buff like Natal. I don't know why but I don't seem to have passionate interests like other people do. I just like everything! My half-sister Juliana is really into art. She's been studying the most famous Spanish painters, so I'm always finding books and web pages that she's been looking at. I'm sure you've heard of Spain's most famous artist. His name was Salvador Dalí. Actually, his full name was much longer: Salvador Domingo Felipe Jacinto Dalí i Domènech. What a mouthful! The name Salvador didn't originally belong to him, either. Dalí was born 9 months after his big brother had died. The brother was called Salvador, too. Dalí's parents told him that he was the reincarnation of his brother. What a strange thing to say to a young boy!

When he was famous, the King of Spain gave him a title. He was the Marqués de Dalí de Púbol. The King respected him very much and even visited Dalí when he was on his deathbed. Dalí's work is very well known, but I think it's strange. Have you seen it? Dalí is known for art in the Cubist, Surrealist, and Dadaist styles. One of his most famous paintings has clocks that look like they're melting. Another one has animals with long, twiggy legs and they're walking high up in the sky. Dali looked strange too. He had a long moustache that he waxed so it would stand straight, like knitting needles.

Picasso: Not Just a Painter

Another Spanish painter you might have heard of is Pablo Picasso, whose full name was completely crazy! It was Pablo Diego José Francisco de Paula Juan Nepomuceno María de los Remedios Cipriano de la Santísima Trinidad Ruiz y Picasso. That's way too long, don't you think? Many people think that Picasso was French because he spent a long time living in France, but actually he was Spanish. Picasso was born in Málaga, Spain in 1881. He wasn't just a painter, though. Picasso was also a printmaker, sculptor, ceramicist, poet, stage designer, and playwright. I don't know how he found the time! But painting was his main interest. When he was very young, his father gave him lessons on copying the artistic masters.

Fun Fact

Picasso's mother said that his first word was 'piz', short for 'lapiz', the spanish word for pencil!

Picasso is known for his wacky paintings, but he has painted in all different styles. You'll probably recognise his Cubist paintings, where everything looks like blocks and squares, even people's faces. Many of his portraits make people look strange. Some have eyes in the top of their heads or long, droopy noses. I don't think I'd be very flattered by a painting like that, even if it was done by a famous person! Juliana loves Picasso's work and has some posters of his work on her wall. She wants to visit the Museu Picasso in Barcelona. There are three other museums about Picasso in Spain. Two are in Málaga, where the artist was born. But there are three Picasso museums in France, and one in Germany, too. I suggested to Juliana that she could do a tour of all the Picasso museums for an international holiday. She just rolled her eyes and said she'd never be able to afford that. I said she should become a famous artist like Picasso and then she'd just need to sell one painting to go on the trip. Guess what? That made Juliana roll her eyes even more. Sisters!

Where do you like to go on holiday? To be honest, I don't go to many places. Whenever I have time off, I go to visit Padre. Toledo, where Padre lives with Natal, is a city. Puebla de Sanabria, where I usually live, is a village. I guess I get the best of both worlds. My step-sister Juliana is getting older now and soon she will leave home and live somewhere else or go to university. Once Juliana has left home, it will be easier for me to take a holiday with Madre and Matias. Juliana is always fussy about

Bustling Barcelona

I want to go on holiday to Barcelona. It's a popular place for local and international tourists in Spain. The Basilica of the Sagrada Familia is one of the best things to see in Barcelona. It's an amazing church that started to be built in the 1800s. Guess what? It's still not finished! The church is so amazing that it has taken years to put together, and they guess it might be finished in 2040 or something. Actually, it's not a church, but a cathedral. The carvings on the outside of the building are so amazing. It's impossible to appreciate all the little details of the architecture. Fun Fact: The Basilica of the Sagrada Familia has incredibly tall towers.

Casa Batlló, locally known as Casa dels ossos, meaning "House of Bones" is one of Antoni Gaudí's masterpieces. It is located in the center of Barcelona along Illa de la Discòrdia, a row of houses made by other Modernista architects of Barcelona.

Antoni Gaudí: Architect Extraordinaire

If you like fantastic architecture, when in Barcelona you should also see Casa Batlló. This building is a masterpiece of Antoni Gaudí, an architect who also worked on the famous basilica. The Batlló family wanted a house that would stand out and be unique in town. They didn't want to have a house like any other, and so encouraged Gaudí to create a risky and unusual design. From the outside, the house is colorful and wonky. The windows were refurbished in unusual shapes that curve and wind across the building. I've heard that the inside is amazing, too.

Another Gaudí masterpiece to visit is Parc Guell. This park in Barcelona is of special interest to me since I've been helping Mr. Sanchez in his garden. Most people will be interested in the architecture in the park but I think there must be some amazing trees and flowers to see, too.

Fun Fact

Casa Batlló is one of the inspirations in the rabbit burrows of the animated film *Zootopia*.

Peaceful Islands

Madre doesn't like big cities any more. She'd rather go to small places or visit islands. She's really taken to village life! I know that Madre wants to go to the Cies Islands. The islands are an archipelago which means a chain or group of islands. Islas Cies have been a nature reserve since 1980, and people say they are very beautiful. Not many tourists go there. Islas Cíes consist of three islands. The first one is called Monteagudo, which means 'Sharp Mount' or North Island. Then there's do Faro which means 'Lighthouse Island,' or it can be called Isla do Medio, the Middle Island. Finally, San Martiño is Saint Martin or South Island. You can go camping but you need to book ahead. They limit how many people can camp to protect the island. On Monteagudo Island there is a beach called Rodas, which was once named the most beautiful beach in the world.

Hiking Tourism

Matias, my step-father, likes to go hiking. If he has a day off work and the weather is fine, he asks Madre to make him a picnic and he goes hiking by himself. He doesn't invite anyone else because Matias walks very fast. I don't think I could keep up with him. I know he wants to go on a hiking holiday sometime. A great place in Spain to go climbing is in the Spanish Pyrenees. Matias has been reading about a place called Ainsa which is just south of the Pyrenees. He said there is a medieval village where you can get great views of the forests. Another historic city in the area is called La Seu D'Urgell. I'm sure it's a nice place to go on holiday, but Matias will have to wait until I'm older and my legs are longer! Then I'd be happy to go hiking.

Palacio Real de Madrid

Visiting the Capital

Madrid is the capital of Spain. I've been there once or twice before when I was younger, but I can't remember what I did. Juliana went there on a school trip last year. She visited the Prado National Museum. The Prado has one of the largest art collections in the world. They don't just have Spanish artwork, but also Italian, French, and Flemish paintings. Many of the old paintings are religious. Juliana knows all about them. She really likes tryptic paintings, which are paintings that are done on three boards. Usually there is one big one in the middle, and two smaller ones either side.

The Royal Palace of Madrid is another popular place to visit. The palace is in the rococo style and has over 2,000 gilded rooms. Gilded means to be covered in a thin layer of gold. I imagine those golden rooms sparkle when its sunny! I'd like to go to the Naval Museum. Because I'm Rio, I like things to do with water. Rivers are more interesting than the sea, but I like looking at old boats. The craftsmanship is incredible. I like to imagine what it was like to sail across the ocean on one of those old wooden boats. Don't you think it would be terrifying?

44

CONCLUSION

Well my friends, it's time to say goodbye, or adios. Have you enjoyed learning about Spain? It's been fun telling you about my country. I've learned so much as well! I hope it's been interesting. It's hard to know what everyone will like. Some people like museums or gardening, some like animals or architecture, some like food and some like learning about traditions and customs. Whatever you like, I hope there's been something interesting for you to learn about Spain.

My country is a great place to visit. It's fun and vibrant, and I'm sure you'll have a good visit. I wonder what you'll think about the food? If you ask me, it's delicious! Try to remember the names of everything you try so that you can tell you friends back home. In my opinion, everybody should come to Spain! Well, enjoy! Adios!

Which parts of Spain did you like the most and why?

_____

_____

_____

_____

_____

_____

_____

_____

_____

_____

_____

What activities did you enjoy most and why?

_____

_____

_____

_____

_____

_____

_____

_____

_____

_____

_____

Now, to our pop quiz! Good luck!

Spain's full name is 'The Kingdom of Spain' – how do you say this in Spanish?
a) Kingdom de España
b) Reino de España
c) Rey de España

(answer (b) – Reino de España)

In Málaga, in the south of Spain, which month is the coldest?
a) November
b) December
c) January

(answer (c) – January)

Conquistador Hernán Cortés was responsible for the fall of which empire?

a) The Aztec Empire
b) The Inca Empire
c) The Mayan Empire

(answer (a) – The Aztec Empire)

Which of these carnivores, common in Spain, is the most endangered?
a) European polecat
b) Eurasian
c) Iberian wolf

(answer (c) – Iberian wolf, whose conservation status is vulnerable?)

Which of these endemic Spanish birds is now extinct?
a) Balearic warbler
b) Canary Islands oystercatcher
c) Tenerife blue chaffinch

(answer (b) – Canary Islands oystercatcher)

What is the second longest river in Spain, measuring 910km (565 miles) long?
a) Duero River
b) Miño River
c) Ebro River

(answer (c) –Ebro River)

On what date did the temperature in Calamocha drop to −30 °C?
a) January 5, 1983
b) December 17, 1963
c) December 29, 2004

(answer (b) – December 17, 1963)

Isabella of Castile reigned until her death, in which year?
a) 1460
b) 1504
c) 1532

(answer (b) – 1504)

In Spain, what gift would the groom traditionally give to the bride's father after the marriage proposal?
a) A bunch of flowers
b) A car
c) A watch

(answer (c) – A watch)

How do you say Merry Christmas in Spanish?
a) Feliz Navidad
b) Merii Kurisumasu
c) Buon Natale

(answer (a) – Feliz Navidad)